Mental Manipulation

Powerful Techniques in the Dark Psychology. Persuading and Influencing People With Mind Control, Brainwash and NLP

By Victor Murphy

Legal Disclaimer

The information contained in this book and its contents is not designed to replace any form of medical or professional advice; and is not meant to replace the need for independent medical, financial, legal, or other professional advice or services that may be required. The content and information in this book have been provided for educational and entertainment purposes only.

The content and information contained in this book have been compiled from sources deemed reliable, and they are accurate to the best of the Author's knowledge, information, and belief. However, the Author cannot guarantee its accuracy and validity and therefore cannot be held liable for any errors and/or omissions. Further, changes are periodically made to this book as needed. Where appropriate and/or necessary, you must consult a professional (including but not limited to your doctor, attorney, financial advisor, or other such professional) before using any of the suggested remedies, techniques, and/or information in this book.

Upon using this book's contents and information, you agree to hold harmless the Author from any damages, costs, and expenses, including any legal fees, potentially resulting from the application of any of the information in this book. This disclaimer applies to any loss, damages, or injury caused by the use and application of this book's contents, whether directly or indirectly, whether for breach of contract, tort, negligence, personal injury, criminal intent, or under any other circumstance.

You agree to accept all risks of using the information presented in this book.

You agree that by continuing to read this book, where appropriate and/or necessary, you shall consult a professional (including but not limited to your doctor, attorney, financial advisor, or other such professional) before using any of the suggested remedies, techniques, or information in this book.

Table of Contents

Introduction

Not every person you meet has good intentions. That's a rather negative statement to start a book, but it's a truth that we all need to learn.

You might be a kind-hearted, open-minded person, someone who is happy to communicate and interact with anyone, provided they are interesting and happy to be in your presence. The problem is, that person might have an agenda, other thoughts on their mind, and there is no way of you knowing about this until you're possibly in too deep.

This book is about mental manipulation, which is also widely known as emotional manipulation or psychological manipulation. It is a form of abuse in so many ways, and it can occur within relationships, friendships, family links, or at work. The most common situations for this type of manipulation to occur is in romantic relationships and work-based situations, however.

Someone who has dealt with this type of manipulation often needs time to deal with the effects of the abuse afterward, be it through therapy or a little soul-searching in private. The bottom line is that mental manipulation of any kind is damaging and something which it's important you understand and know the signs of, in order to spot it before it becomes a deep-rooted problem in your life.

You've probably heard the word 'narcissist' and in many ways that's what this book is also about. A narcissist uses mental manipulation on a regular basis to get what he or she wants, and it's so subtle and thinly veiled that it so often goes unnoticed until it builds up into an avalanche of effects.

This book is about the entire spectrum of mental manipulation. We're going to cover the basics of what it is, how it's done, who might use it, how it might affect you, and we're going to talk about how to spot if it's actually happening to you now. From there, we'll get positive and pro-active and talk about how to stop it from happening to you again.

If you've ever been a victim of this type of emotional abuse, you'll know first-hand just how upsetting and world-altering it can be. It can change the way you feel about yourself, the way you feel about the world, it can give you serious trust and intimacy issues and it cause you to wonder whether you're actually going crazy. The truth is, you're not, you're being manipulated in a very clever but very devious way.

So, let's begin delving into this rather murky world, and learn more about mental manipulation as a whole.

Chapter 1
What is Mental Manipulation?

We all know what manipulation means. This is usually a tactic employed to try to get another person to do something you want them to do. You do this by either promising them something, blackmailing them, twisting their words, making them see that what you want them to do is a good idea, there are countless ways to manipulate.

Manipulation is never a positive thing because you're taking away someone's free will and not allowing them to think for themselves or do what they feel is right.

Mental manipulation is less about blackmail and promises, and far more about twisting that person's logic and making them feel that they have to do something or have to feel or say something because it's the right thing to do. Of course, there is black magic at work here in some ways, because when you are mentally manipulating someone, you're causing them to question their own logic. You're tricking their brain into thinking that something else is a good idea. The problem is their intuition will be screaming at them that it's not. That's where the inner turmoil comes in.

A person who is being mentally manipulated usually knows something isn't quite right, but they can't put their finger on it, or they don't want to put their finger on it. The best example here is a person who is head over heels in love with someone who is also a narcissist. A narcissist is someone who happily tramples over whoever they like to get what they want. Of course, we should point out that genuine Narcissistic Personality Disorder, or NPD, is actually quite rare. Despite that, there are many people out there (more than you would like to know about) who display extremely narcissistic tendencies and are basically not the nicest people to know. They are deceiving, they are wolves in sheep clothing, and they can cause a whole world of emotional pain and upset to someone who is in the grips of their control.

Mental Manipulation And The Narcissist
Why would someone fall in love with a person like this? Well, they don't show that at first. A narcissist, whether true or

otherwise, is the epitome of charm at the very beginning. You see, this type of person is very insecure at their very core, and in order to cover that up, they act confident, brash, charming, like the most amazing man or women you've ever met. They will shower you with gifts, compliments, make you feel like the most treasured person on Earth, and then it will begin.

The most common situation in which a narcissist, in particular, will try and use mental manipulation on a partner is if they feel they are about to leave. It's not uncommon for a person to try and end a relationship with a narcissist because they come to the end of their tether. In this case, they will end the relationship and the partner being left will twist everything around, will cause the other person to start to question their decision, they will use manipulative techniques that cause them to question their own logic and sanity, and they're basically playing games with someone's psychological wellbeing.

There is no fun in being with a person who uses any type of manipulation, be it mental or otherwise.

Of course, it's not just narcissists that use manipulation of this kind. Anyone can use it; a person you might think wonderful things about might suddenly go through a hard time and start acting out. This might cause them to panic about what is happening to them and as a result, they resort to low tactics to keep others in their lives. This is when mental manipulation might come into play.

As a side point, if you want to learn more about narcissists, this is something we will be exploring a little more in our next chapter.

Raising Awareness of a Tough Subject
From this first section, you can probably tell that a person who has been subjected to mental, emotional, and psychological manipulation of any degree can be very damaged and scarred by it. Not everyone manages to recognize what is happening and get away from the situation, there are countless people in relationships which are extremely manipulative but they can't find the strength to leave. It's a terrible and upsetting thing to think about.

This book is designed to raise awareness of what mental manipulation is, what it looks like, and what it isn't love, no matter how you dress it up and twist around. Someone who loves you will never make you question your sanity, no matter how difficult things get.

You might think we're focusing unfairly on relationships here and not really talking about other situations which mental manipulation might come into, e.g. work situations, but the truth is that the overwhelming number of situations are more likely to be romantic than anything else. The reason this type of manipulation is so damaging in this case is that emotions are so involved. When emotions aren't really that deeply connected, e.g. perhaps in a work situation, the manipulation is far easier to spot and deal with. When you've fallen in love someone, you don't want to believe that they're capable of these terrible things, so of course, you push your suspicions down and you try and see the good in them.

This can only go on for so long.

This chapter is designed to bring your attention to the subject and really introduce you to what we need to discuss in greater detail. In our next chapter we're going to delve deeper and talk about how someone might use manipulation of this kind, the types of tactics they might employ, and the dynamics of it all. The aim at this point is that you can understand the severity of what mental manipulation means to someone who is in the middle of it all. Not quite blind to it, but keeping their eyes half closed, even if they do have a suspicion. The hope at the end of this book is that if you are someone who is being mentally manipulated in this way, by a narcissist or anyone else, you'll recognize the signs and you'll find the strength to leave.

Let's move onto our next chapter and delve deeper into the dynamics of this subject.

Chapter 2

Understanding The

Dynamics of Emotional

Manipulation

Now we've introduced you to what mental manipulation is and we've explained why it's so damaging, let's get practical and really delve into the inner workings of this type of situation.

From the outside looking in, it's easy to wonder why someone would fall for a manipulative trick. You could say the same about any situation because when you're not in it, it's easy to question and judge it. As we mentioned in our last chapter when emotions are involved, these can often cloud your common sense and judgment, and they make you weak to see things which you would otherwise spot a mile away.

Some manipulators are better than others. It's not unheard of for a friend or family member to be warning a person about their significant other, telling them that they're not acting in a decent way, that they're manipulating them, they're being emotionally abusive, but will that person listen? No. They will not listen until they have realized it for themselves, and that can be heartbreaking to watch. The other situation is that the manipulator is a pro, and they fool everyone, even those looking in. Both are dangerous, but the after effects of the second type are usually harder to understand for all those involved.

Traits of a Manipulator

As we've just mentioned some manipulators are better at it than others, and it's not easy to spot one at first. It's normally only after the event that you can see the red flags, but let's discuss the main personality traits of a manipulative person. Hopefully, this might raise a few warning lights if you are someone currently being manipulated without your conscious knowledge.

- Often seem the epitome of perfection and charm at first
- Quite selfish, only really care about getting their needs met, and usually, truly believe that their needs are more important than anyone else's

- May get caught up in their lies because they tell so many

- Anger can often flare up quite easily

- Can swing from aggressive and name calling to calm and apologizing quickly

- Quite controlling, especially if in a relationship

- Have little regard or understanding of boundaries

- Shirks or avoids responsibilities

- Will often turn the blame around onto the other person

- Great at identifying someone's weaknesses and using them against them

- Often talk about others behind their backs

- Rarely do what they say they will

Again, looking at that list you might wonder why anyone would get involved with such a terrible person, but these traits rarely come to the fore at first! In addition, the types of mental manipulation used help to mask these traits and minimize them, or make the other person believe that it's actually them in the wrong, and not the manipulator.

Nobody can really understand what it is likely to be manipulated in this way unless it has happened to them. Not really knowing whether you're seeing things as they are, you're paranoid, you're thinking wrong of someone, these are all thoughts that will pop into the head of someone who is being emotionally abused, and that is what mental manipulation is - abuse, pure and simple. The mechanics of mental manipulation, i.e. the way it works, is so subtle that it's hard to spot until it becomes unbearable. In that case, the victim of it all will either crack completely or walk away for good.

Many of the traits we've mentioned above are classic narcissistic traits too. We have mentioned narcissists a few times already but it's certainly a good point to bring it up in more detail here.

A true narcissist is someone who has a personality disorder, called NPD. In this case, the person 100% truly believes that their actions are right and orderly. This person is thinking in a disordered way because of their condition. This doesn't mean what they are doing is excused, but it is a personality disorder problem which requires therapy and treatment in order to overcome it. The sad truth is that most narcissistic people will not seek treatment, because they do not believe there is anything wrong with them - they think there is something wrong with everyone else. For this reason, most narcissists remain alone, because having a relationship or forming close friendships with a person like this is quite damaging for the other person involved.

On the other hand, the majority of people we would label narcissists do not have a personality disorder, they simply display traits of a narcissist. Is this excusable? Not at all. A person who shows narcissistic traits needs to face up to their issues and behavior and learn to get past them, in order to stop damaging those around them and in order to have valuable and fulfilling relationships in the future. Again, the problem is that most never do this, because they are full of self-importance.

A narcissist, whether true or not, believes that they are the best at everything, their opinion is right and everyone else's opinion is wrong. They believe that they can do no wrong and that the people in their lives should bend to their will. They will seem charming and wonderful at first, but once they have you under their spell, the deception will begin.

Why Does Someone Choose to Use Mental Manipulation?

Unless you are in the head of a person using this type of tactic, it's hard to really pinpoint it down. In the case of a narcissistic, a person with a true personality disorder, it's simply because that is how they operate. That is how they believe they should get what they want, that they have a right to do this because they're not wrong.

Another reason for someone opting to use mental manipulation tactics is out of fear. If this is part and parcel of a romantic relationship and they see their partner perhaps doing better than them, maybe in their career, maybe they've had an image overhaul and people are looking at them with admiration, or some other change which has caused the other person to feel threatened and worried that they might leave, they may manipulate them into staying through unfair means. They say that all is fair in love and war, and there are countless examples of people using manipulation in order to get a partner to stay with them, or to get them to be 'dumbed down'.

A person who uses this type of tactic is quite insecure at their very core. They will see their partner improving themselves and they won't see it as a positive. Someone who would never dream of using manipulation would see their partner in this situation and be proud of them, pat them on the back and say 'well done'. Not a manipulator. In this case, they will do whatever they can to get them back in their box and close the lid. They do not like change, they like things to remain as they are, and that normally means that they are the one in control.

There is no way to legitimize any type of manipulation, but these are a couple of examples when it may come into play, and two of the most common. It could also simply be that this person is simply a bad apple. It happens, unfortunately. A partner might do their best to see the good in them, and they will give them enough of a flicker to hang onto, but the rest of their behavior is far from positive, and far more manipulative than they might admit to.

The Power of Gas Lighting

Have you heard of gaslighting? This is a tactic which is used to manipulate and make someone question their own sanity. This is also a tactic which is very closely linked to narcissistic behavior, as it is one of the top methods used by this type of person.

Gaslighting is extremely dangerous but also extremely subtle. It's hard for the victim to see what is happening at the time, and a person who is quite good at gaslighting, i.e. a narcissist, will be able to successfully make this person truly believe that they are actually losing their mind. By doing that, the victim is effectively 'put in their place', meaning they won't leave. Job is done for the narcissist or manipulator. This is a class tactic used in emotionally abusive relationships especially, although can happen in any other type of connection, such as family, work situations, or friendships. Again, it is likely to be far more damaging in a romantic relationship because of the deep emotions involved.

Gaslighting is done slowly and subtly, which makes it even more powerful. The common ways to adopt gas lighting include:

- **Telling quite obvious lies** - You know that the person is lying to you, but they're so blatant with it that you can't quite believe it's true. Would they really be that obvious? You're questioning yourself by even asking that question. The idea here is to keep you constantly doubting, constantly off-kilter and that is why the lie is done in such an obvious way. By doing this, they can get away with anything.

- **They deny what you know they have said** - You might 100% know that you heard something they said, but they will deny it ever came out of their mouth. This in itself gets you thinking 'did I really hear that right?', 'am I imagining it?' The more you start to question what you know to be true, the more you're buying into their version of reality.

- **They use things close to you** - A manipulator using gaslighting tactics will deal a low blow and use the things you love against you. For instance, if your career is important to you, they might say something like 'they promoted you because the other person was sick on interview day' or something similar. It basically makes you question the closest things to you, and by doing that you're questioning your own identity.

- **They say things but don't do them** - The 'actions speak louder than words' adage is true here. It's best to look at their actions rather than listening to their words because the two do not match. A victim might cling onto their words however, desperate not to believe what they are starting to suspect is really happening.

- **They change their behavior to keep you** - After a period of particularly negative behavior, you might notice that they suddenly start to be loving. This is to help you see the good and to stop you from leaving. This is to keep you off balance, always questioning whether you imagined the bad things or not. Surely they couldn't be that bad? That's what you're left thinking.

- **They blame you for what they are doing** - If you suspect they are cheating on you, they're probably going to deny it until they're blue in the face, but then accuse you of doing the same. This is partly their insecurities and guilt, but another way of getting you to question your own sanity and therefore distract your mind from what they are doing.

- **They make you think everyone is against you** - A person using gaslighting techniques will make you believe that those closest to you are against you too. Lines like 'she knows you can't cook very well' when talking about your mother who you just cooked Sunday dinner for, or 'she knows you're terrible at your job, but she's just being polite' about your close colleague. By doing this you're questioning those closest to you, your support network, and that in itself alienates you and isolates you from everyone around you.

- **They tell you that those around you are lying** - By telling you that other people are lying, they're isolating you once more. Once they have you alone, without a support network around you, you're more vulnerable. This is another way of distorting your own version of reality and buying into theirs.

From that list, you can see how damaging gaslighting can be. It makes you question your sanity and your own reality, it makes you push away those closest to you and takes away your support network. Gaslighting is a master manipulator tactic and one of the most deeply damaging psychologically. When you don't believe your own logic and your own sanity, you have lost yourself, and that means you're floating around, desperate to cling onto something strong and solid - in that case, you're likely to cling onto the manipulator, who is then able to dig their claws in even deeper.

How Does it Make The Victim Feel?

There are likely to be many thoughts and feelings going around a victim's head but confused is probably the main one.

Most people who have been a victim to mental manipulation know deep down that something isn't quite right, perhaps a nagging voice or intuitive thought that it screaming 'don't listen', but it's on mute or isn't quite loud enough. It could very well be that this person knows what they're dealing with, but they're not quite ready to go. They still hang onto the thought that this person has some good in them, perhaps that they can save them.

You cannot save or right the actions of a person who uses mental manipulation as a control tactic. The only thing you can do is walk away. Of course, that is far easier said than done.

We've mentioned before that a person who has undergone a period of manipulation of this kind is quite likely to be emotionally scarred and damaged once the ordeal is over. It may be that they never feel that they want to connect to another person again, they may develop severe trust issues, and they may also find it extremely difficult to be intimate with another person in the future.

It's important for a person who has been subject to abuse of this kind to seek professional help to allow them to unpick what has happened and really solidify in their mind the facts. Even years afterward it's not unusual for a person to not quite 100% believe what happened. They might still have some glimmer of thinking they were wrong, or that they might have imagined something. It's important to go through a professional route and really get to the heart of what happened. This is important for future relationships and future happiness because otherwise, the whole cycle is likely to repeat itself.

Many victims of manipulation also develop anxiety, depression, or even PTSD (post-traumatic stress disorder), depending on how severe the experience was.

Whilst the ordeal is actually happening, aside from confusion, the constant questioning of their own sanity can cause a person to shrink into themselves. In this case, they might stop going out, stop seeing friends, and therefore cut themselves off from those who are open to helping them. They may become depressed, lose interest in their work, and have no hope for the future. This is exactly the outcome that a manipulator wants because when this happens, they really do have the victim under their thumb, and he or she is not going anywhere.

Put simply, mental manipulation can, in some cases, destroy a person.

What's Really Going on Under The Surface

So, underneath all of this, what is really happening? Is this person evil? Do they want to watch someone they claim to care about whither away to nothing?

Nobody can tell, but in most cases, it's not really that sinister. We mentioned narcissists before, and a person with true NPD doesn't actually want to ruin or destroy another person, they simply cannot understand why they can't see things from their side. They are literally at a loss to understand why this person is not understanding their level of self-importance.

There are many different types of narcissists, ranging from mild to moderate, and some a little more severe, but there is one particular type which basically cannot be saved without extreme therapy. This is the malignant narcissist.

A malignant narcissist is a sociopath, some might even say psychopath in some cases, and they will twist, turn, manipulate, deceive, and ruin another person for their own gains. The terrifying thing about this type of narcissist is that most will never seek treatment because they are so deeply into themselves that they really can't see anything wrong. Whilst we're not suggesting all narcissists of this kind are going to go out and commit a terrible crime against another person, there have been instances in the past where serial killers or other criminals have been unearthed to have malignant narcissistic personalities.

How can you tell if you're in the midst of one? You probably won't until it's too late, and when you do realize what's going on, you need to get away as quickly as possible. In this case, you will probably need emotional support afterward, to understand what happened and to help you realize that none of it was your fault, that you really weren't going crazy.

At the midst of it all, that is what a victim is going to feel like - that they are going crazy, and that in itself is a terrible, out of control, feeling. The fact is that a manipulator feeds off of this vulnerability because they are so lacking in their own confidence and self-worth.

This chapter has covered a lot of ground in terms of the dynamics of what goes in a manipulative situation such as this, and what types of tactics may be used. We ended the chapter by talking about a rather worrying type of narcissist. Now, do not worry about this too much. Manipulative narcissists are quite rare, but it's important to highlight their existence when talking about the very subject that this type of person lives for.

Nobody can 100% tell you why a person would be mentally manipulative towards another. We can speculate and give examples of why it has happened in the past, but as of yet, we are unable to get into another person's head and really examine their thoughts! Perhaps when that type of technology comes we will learn more about this type of behavior but for now, it's best to focus on awareness. This means understanding what techniques are used, being able to spot them, and learning how to deal with the experience and kick it out of your life. Of course, in most situations, this also means walking away from the person who is causing you such mental anguish.

Chapter 3

How Manipulators Use Neuro-Linguistic Programming to Change Your Thought Processes

The human brain works in confusing and complicated ways, with various pathways connecting our thoughts, emotions, and what we perceive reality to be. Of course, you can train your brain to think or feel anything if you focus on it for long enough, and at the heart of all psychological processes, including cognitive behavioral therapy (CBT) is that very type of brain training.

There is however a form of training which can be used for good but can also be misused for bad. This is called Neuro-linguistic programming, or NLP for short.

Whether or not a manipulator has inside knowledge of what they are doing psychologically or whether it is simply a tactic they feel works from the reactions of the person they're close to remains to be seen, but NLP is regularly used to manipulate a victim into questioning their reality, and therefore questioning their own sanity. Is gaslighting a form of NLP? In some ways, but we'll talk about that in a short while in a little more detail. NLP in itself is a quite subtle and complex process, but an extremely effective way to alter someone's thought processes, simply by using clever words and phrases.

What is Neuro-Linguistic Programming (NLP)?

NLP sounds confusing, but the title is quite misleading. Anyone can learn NLP, which means it can be used for good and bad. We should point out here and now that at its very core, NLP is supposed to be used as self-development and improvement tool, it is not supposed to be used as a way to control others. Unfortunately, some unscrupulous types have learned how to use this very technique for bad rather than good.

First things first, let's explain what NLP actually is.

NLP was founded back in the 1970s by Richard Bandler and John Grinder. This is a way of communicating with the mind. The idea behind NLP is that there is a direct link between language and behavior, with the brain's neurological processes, e.g. thoughts and suggestion.

NLP can be used for good reasons, e.g. it has been used to help with depression, learning disorders, phobias, and damaging habits. This is all done by controlling the mind, i.e. telling it what you want it to do and persuading it, via your words, to do that exact thing.

NLP works because it taps into patterns. If you think about your general life, you probably have a pattern for everything, e.g. how you get up in the mornings, how you go to bed, how you eat, how you prepare to go out in the evenings. We are creatures of habit. These habits are formed because there is a chemical reaction between the thoughts that our mind conjure up and the things we do. This means that every action in that pattern is performed because of a thought, which can either be conscious or it can be unconscious, i.e. not something you're aware of. NLP, therefore, uses patterns and words to train the brain to think or do a certain thing.

NLP can help change the way you see the world, and that sentence in itself tells you why manipulators effectively use this technique to trap someone in a particular pattern of thinking. Remember, our feelings and our thoughts are what create our own version of reality, and when these are altered, our version of reality is also altered.

Two positive and useful NLP exercises include:

Disassociation

This particular Technique is ideal for helping to get rid of a particular emotion or feeling that you find troubling.

Disassociation means identifying the thing you want to get rid of, i.e. shyness, and then identifying the emotion which goes along with it, so nervousness perhaps in this case. You would then close your eyes and imagine yourself floating above your body, and seeing the situation from the outside, looking in. You will notice that you feel different about it instantly because it's not happening to you at that moment. Using this technique when situations peak is a great way to avoid negative emotions from taking hold.

Reframing

Reframing means identifying a negative that you constantly tell yourself and giving it an alternative explanation, i.e. a positive slant. For instance, maybe you lose your job. Firstly that is terrible and you're going to feel bad for a while, but you can reframe your emotions by coming up with something positive and putting it on repeat. In this situation, you might think about the fact you can retrain and finally do the one thing you've always wanted to do. This allows you to see negative experiences as less life-changing and terrible, and simply as ways to change direction and perhaps learn.

There are countless other NLP exercises and it's really something that you need to dedicate time to in order to learn how it can be useful to you. What we need to explore however is how the language of your brain and influencing it can be used against you, i.e. in the hands of a manipulator.

You might be looking at those two exercises and wonder how a manipulator could use them for negative, but these are simple explanations of what this technique is about. By reading about these techniques you can understand that you're influencing your thoughts by telling your brain what you want it to think and therefore believe. We act on our thoughts, so your actions will mirror what you're thinking.

When a manipulator constantly tells you something, i.e. "you're useless", the more you hear it, the more you start to believe it. In the end, your actions start to mirror your thoughts. So, you'll start doing less, trying less, not reaching out for new opportunities, and in the end, your manipulator has won, because you're dumbed down, firmly in their clutches.

The human brain also learns by repetition. Think back to when you were a child and you were learning the alphabet. Can you remember the alphabet song? Of course you can, you all sang it several times during a school day! The reason you can still remember it is because of that repetitive action that your school teacher imparted on you. In some ways, that's NLP. We learn via NLP techniques. So, when you hear negative phrases about yourself from someone you trust and care about, your brain believes them.

So, to sum up, NLP is a way of communicating with the mind and changing the thoughts that it creates, therefore changing actions at the same time. It's supposed to be a positive technique to help people get over difficult situations and negative emotions, but in the wrong hands, it can be used with very damaging consequences.

Is NLP Used to Brainwash?

In some ways, yes. NLP in many ways is mind control because you're controlling what you want your mind to believe. Whilst you're not hypnotizing someone and forcing them under your will, you're doing it in a more subtle way. In the end, the brain will believe what it is constantly being told, so if someone is in the clutches of a very clever manipulator and they are being told a certain thing daily, it's quite likely that they will firmly believe that to be their reality.

Remember that we mentioned earlier about patterns, i.e. we do things in patterns and that's how our brain knows what to expect. A manipulator using NLP uses patterns via the art of repetition. It's a constant drip of information, a constant feeding of what they want you to believe. Of course, it's a false story; you're not useless, they just want you to believe that because the moment you realize your potential, you're likely to go off trying to better yourself and that takes you away from them. Remember, at the very heart of it all, a manipulator is a self-involved person who is severely lacking in confidence. They want you where they can see you and control you because then you're not going anywhere.

If you look at propaganda used in political campaigns or for other uses, it is in some ways used to brainwash people into believing what they are being told. The clever selection of words and images to go along with the speech is used to help the person see that the way they're being shown is the right way. This fosters a belief and faithfulness towards the cause, which is often unshakeable. Is this NLP? Yes, in some ways it is. So if we're asking whether NLP is a form of brainwashing, then when it is in the wrong hands, it can be.

Is Gas Lighting a Form of NLP?

Whilst gaslighting is a tactic on its own, it is an indirect form of NLP because you're tricking someone into thinking their reality is wrong, and yours is right. Again, it's like propaganda but done in a subtle and slow way. The reason that gaslighting is so effective and therefore so damaging is because of the slow way it is done. This flies under the radar and isn't detected until it's too late.

We know that NLP is a way of communicating with the brain and changing thoughts and therefore actions. Gaslighting is a method of getting someone to question their sanity and their beliefs, and when done successfully, that person is likely to believe the manipulator's version of reality instead of their own. That is brainwashing, that is NLP, and therefore manipulators are using NLP, a very sophisticated form of psychology against their victims without their knowledge.

Can you see how terrifying and damaging manipulation can be? You're not simply forcing someone to do something they don't want to do, which is bad enough on its own, but you're tricking them and changing their thoughts and emotions too. You're taking away their overall control and identity. Manipulation is a cruel business, but it's one which happens so commonly because when it is done well, it is too subtle to notice until it's too late.

How to Recognise NLP in Practice
Recognizing NLP whilst it is happening is very, very difficult. The reason is that you're

not really on the lookout for it in the general routine of life. Nobody goes around wondering whether someone is intentionally making them question their own sanity, it's not something we would ever imagine would happen to us, especially by someone we care about. For this reason, many people are manipulated by NLP techniques without even knowing it. For many, however, its those outside of the situation who spots it first.

For instance, two people are in a relationship and one partner is narcissistic. They are manipulating the other partner by using gaslighting techniques and constantly telling them that they're terrible at their job. They tell them constantly, with small jibes and remarks and suggesting they should change their career and perhaps work from home instead. This is a constant stream of attack, but it's done so subtly that the victim cannot see it.

However, the victim's sister might have suspicions about what is happening, because she doesn't see her sibling much anymore and they seem different. She can see beyond the adoration the victim feels for the abusive partner, but she's not sure how to approach this sensitive subject without it backfiring.

In most cases, an outside influence spots the NLP in progress before the person concerned. This is because the person in the middle of it is being tricked, and when the mind is involved, it's very hard to separate fact from fiction.

In our next chapter we're going to talk about how to protect yourself from NLP and other manipulative tactics, but for now we need to mention that if you have any suspicion at all that a partner, friend, family member, colleague or anyone else in your life is using such mind-related tactics to manipulate you, question it and don't force yourself to believe that it's all in your head. If you have an inkling that means your intuition is screaming at you to listen. You are not paranoid; if you really believe something is going on, even if you think it for a second, then you have to dig a little deeper and examine what is going on with a different viewpoint. Ask someone you care about what they think, question the reality that the manipulator is trying to force you to believe, and above all else, believe your inner voice.

We have intuition for a reason. It is there to keep us safe, and whilst most of us have trouble listening and trusting our intuition, that slight doubt, that inkling that you can't quite put your finger on, is a noise to listen to and a sign to examine what is going on with wide open eyes.

Chapter 4

Is Someone Manipulating You?

We ended our last chapter with an urge to listen to your inner voice, your intuition, and to question the reality that a manipulator is trying to get you to believe. Of course, that is easier said than done, especially when deep emotions are involved.

We never want to believe that someone we care about, respect, and look up to is doing something so underhanded and damaging. Trying to understand why a manipulator manipulates people are trying to understand why water is wet. You will never change this type of person, and you will damage yourself in the process of trying to do so. There is a very good reason why most narcissistic people end up alone. It's a sad fact, but unless they are prepared to go through a long process of deep therapy and alter their mindset, this type of person will continue to hurt others over and over again and see no ill will in it.

Realizing that someone close to you might very well be manipulating you isn't a pleasant thought, but it's one that you have to face up to if you really do believe it might be in your life. Of course, this doesn't mean that you should go around constantly questioning everyone's actions and wondering whether they're trying to twist your mind into believing something other than reality. Most people don't attempt to do this, and by thinking that way you're simply going to make yourself crazy. What you should do is be on the lookout for red flags and simply trust yourself enough to know what your reality is, versus someone else's twisted view.

Only For The Weak?

Do you believe that only a weak person, someone who is lacking in self-confidence would be the victim of manipulation? Think about it carefully.

The truth is that absolutely anyone is at risk of being mentally manipulated.

That's a terrifying thought.

Even the strongest mind in the world can be manipulated if they are vulnerable enough in other ways. For instance, if we meet someone and fall in love, we become vulnerable. This means that we are open to manipulation. If we meet someone and we become so impressed with them that we start to see them as a role model or a mentor, we have let them into our lives, past our walls, and we are vulnerable.

The idea that only a mentally weak person can be manipulated is extremely wrong and something which we need to kick out right now. If you have been manipulated in the past, or you believe you might be being manipulated right now, you are not mentally weak. You simply let someone into your life who doesn't deserve you. The fact is that a manipulator is a weak person, not the victim.

How Psychological Manipulation is Done Through Words

In our last chapter, we talked in detail about NLP and how words can be used to change someone's reality and therefore what they feel is their overall identity. But, with actual words, how is this done?

Do you believe the positive first or the negative? The human brain is hard-wired to believe negatives before positives. This goes back to the days of the cavemen and cavewomen, who were always on high alert in case huge predators came after them and ended their days. This created the 'fight or flight' response, which basically means your mind and body is on high alert, looking for danger and threats, ready to run for cover at any moment. It's a survival technique.

Whilst we might be far away from Flintstones' territory right now, that 'fight or flight' response is still very much within us today. That means that we are hard-wired to believe negative things as a way of stopping ourselves from being tricked into thinking positives that turn out to be false. It's a defense mechanism. The problem is, that very defensive mechanism actually forces us to be more vulnerable to the very manipulation that we're trying to avoid. Fight or flight hasn't evolved since the prehistoric days, and that leaves us open to always believing negative words and not the positives.

Of course, this can be changed, and one of the NLP methods we talked about, reframing, helps you to do just that. The problem is unless you have learned how to be a positive person and how to constantly turn negatives into positives, you're open to always believing the downside, before the upside.

How does this work when someone is using words to manipulate you?

If someone is always telling you negative things about yourself, e.g. you're bad at your job, you need to lose weight, everyone knows you're a terrible cook, etc, you're going to believe it. When you add in the repetitive action of how the human brain learns, you've got a pretty toxic combination.

But, surely constant negatives such as this would be obvious? Not particularly. The reason a manipulator is able to sneak past your walls is that they throw just enough positive in there to keep you questioning whether you're the one making it up or not. For instance 'you need to lose weight, but I like your curves' is both negative and positive. The problem is, the negative is the part they really mean, and they've disguised the line enough to get past your defenses. The more they say it, the more you'll believe that you do indeed need to lose weight, and as a result, your self-confidence will whittle down to zero.

That's just one example but you can see how a manipulator uses just enough sweet talking to hide what they are actually trying to do. This is partly why a narcissist is so dangerous. If they were full on terrible to you all the time, you'd simply walk away; you'd throw your hands up and say "I can't do this anymore" and you'd leave. But, they don't allow you to do that because they pepper in enough of the sweet and loving actions you recognize from when you first met them, to get you wondering whether or not you're seeing things that aren't there.

Always listen to the actions and not their words. Words can be anything, anyone can say whatever they want, it doesn't mean they mean them. The problem with words coming from the mouth of a manipulator is that they are cleverly designed to do damage, and they're not designed to make you feel good or cause you to smile.

Signs of Mental Manipulation to Look For

When you're in the middle of a manipulative situation, it can be hard to see the woods for the trees, however, it's worthwhile being aware of the signs of mental manipulation, so you can attempt to extract yourself from a damaging situation. It's also good to know these in case you can see someone else being manipulated. Whilst it's hard to convince someone that manipulation is a part of their life, by pointing out the signs you're doing enough to make them question the situation, and that could be enough to open their eyes.

The main signs of mental manipulation include:

You're Constantly Hearing Lies When You Know The Truth

If someone is telling you they didn't say something or didn't do something, but you know that they did, that's a big red flag. For instance, a partner might tell you they're going out to see their brother, but you happen to bump into their brother in the street and they tell you they never saw them. When you mention this to your partner they tell you that they never said that, they told you they were going to see a friend. It might seem possible, in fact, it is, but it's also quite likely to be a lie. When this is a constant thing, i.e. it's happening a lot and you know you're not wrong, it's a real possibility that this person is manipulating you into believing what they want you to believe, and not what you know to be true.

What They Say And What They Do Are Two Different Things

We've said this a few times already, but always watch actions and don't pay too much attention to words. A person who is manipulating you will tell you exactly what they know you want to hear. For instance, if your partner stays out all night and you suspect they were with someone else, of course, you don't want to hear that they were, you want them to tell you they fell asleep at their cousin's house after watching a film. They know this, and they will tell you this, giving you relief from your anguish. The problem is, they're more likely to have been doing the thing you fear.

It's also likely that a manipulator will promise you the Earth and never give it to you, always disappointing you and letting you down. When you question them on this, they will turn it around on you and make you seem like the unreasonable one, telling you how lucky you are to have them and you don't appreciate them, perhaps. You then start to feel guilty for questioning them, questioning your sanity, and backing down. This will happen again and again, on loop.

They Are Masters at Guilt Tricks

Whenever you mention something they have done wrong or something which is upsetting you, they will turn the whole situation around and make it your fault. They might get upset themselves, cry, get angry, throw something, or question why you're bringing it up. You then feel guilty for even mentioning it, wishing you'd kept quiet, telling yourself that it wasn't a big deal, and kicking yourself for not keeping your mouth shut. This is manipulation to let them get away with whatever they want to do, without any ramifications for their actions.

Everything is Someone Else's Fault - Usually Yours

A manipulator cannot take responsibility for their actions, especially if they are narcissistic. Everything can be blamed on someone else, and most of the time that will be you. A manipulator is fantastic at playing the victim and they have no grasp on consequences for actions. Again, this means they can get away with absolutely anything because they will simply blame it on another person and use their clever words to make you believe it.

They Make You Responsible For Their Moods

If a manipulator is angry, it's your job to fix it; if a manipulator is sad, you have to solve the problem; if a manipulator is happy, you'll simply be glad that there is no major turmoil going on right at that moment. A manipulator makes the victim responsible for every single one of their moods and when it's a negative mood, every single person in that room will know about it. They can't just get on with their day, knowing that they're having a bad one and assuming it will pass, it's far more likely to be a catastrophic mood that everyone has to feel and be sucked into.

Again, this is an extremely narcissistic trait, but it's one that many manipulators will exhibit too. If you're constantly up and down, at the mercy of the manipulator's moods, that's a red flag coming your way.

They Always go One Better Than You

If you have a headache, they have a migraine; if you're hungry, they're starving; if you're tired, they're exhausted. A manipulator will always go one better and make everything about them. Again, we're talking narcissists here. The bottom line is that they are saying something deeper, on a non-verbal level; they're telling you that their needs and problems are far worse than yours, so you need to focus on them and stop complaining about your own. Of course, this isn't the truth at all, but their behavior forces you to think that way. In the end, you might simply stop verbalizing your own needs, because you know theirs will always take precedence.

They Use Your Weaknesses Against You

A manipulator will go to great effort to find out your weaknesses and your vulnerabilities. When they find these out, they will use them against you, pushing your buttons and causing you emotional turmoil. Of course, they'll then be the ones to catch you when you're having a meltdown, which is enough to make you question whether or not you heard what you heard, saw what you did, etc. This is a gaslighting technique which is unfortunately very successful and keeps the victim off-kilter, not really sure what to believe.

If you're noticing these tactics with someone in your life, perhaps it's time to sit up and take notice. Of course, in order for this to add up to true manipulation, there needs to be ticking off boxes on a regular basis. It can be that you notice someone we've just mentioned only once and never again; that's simply a human being making a mistake. On the other hand, if you notice that someone is using one of these tactics, or even more than one, and it's a regular thing, you might very well have a manipulator in your life.

Chapter 5

How to Protect Yourself Against Different Types of Manipulation

First things first, the bad news.

There is no way to make yourself bulletproof against any type of manipulation in your life, ever. If you let someone into your life, e.g. if you fall in love, admire someone, become friends with someone, then you are allowing yourself to be vulnerable in some way. That means that manipulation is always a risk. What you shouldn't do is go around thinking that manipulation is a certainty. Despite the fact we've talked at length about the subject, the fact remains that there are far more good people on the planet than bad.

Despite that, there are some things you can do to help protect yourself against manipulation happening to you. Whilst they don't come with a 100% guarantee, these suggestions will certainly make you stronger, more positive, and more grounded in who you are. If you can do that, you'll be far more unshakeable as a result.

Become More Positive in General

Becoming a generally more positive person will help you be less of a target for negativity. Whilst there is nobody on this planet who can be positive 100% of the time, you can do your best to positive as much as possible. Try the reframing exercise we mentioned in our NLP chapter, and simply try and count your blessings, rather than your worries.

Mindfulness is a great way to become more positive. This is about living in the moment and not always thinking back to the past, or jumping into the future before it's even happened. Learning to be mindful takes time and effort but it will have great benefits for your self-confidence, your mental health, and your inner strength too.

You can start on the path towards mindfulness by appreciating everything that is going on around you, taking a social media detox, and living a slightly more simple way. For instance, on your walk to work, instead of listening to music and powering on, take the time to look at the trees, the color of the leaves, the way the wind feels against your skin, how the clouds look in the sky, etc. The more you do this, the more grounded you will be, and the abler you will be to deal with difficult situations, such as possible manipulation. You could also try meditation if you get on well with mindfulness, which will further strengthen your identity and focus.

Always Question Things Which Seem 'Off'

Listening to your intuition is something we should all learn to do more of, but it takes trust and time. If something simply doesn't feel right, don't ignore the feeling and don't try and shake it off. If someone tells you something that you don't quite agree with, or which makes you feel a little strange, then question that in your mind. Pick it to pieces and examine the motivation behind it and whether or not it really is the truth, or whether someone could be spinning you a line.

It can be hard to do because gaslighting techniques can make you question both sides of the argument, but listening to your intuition will give you a clearer insight into the true motivations of someone and their words/actions.

Your intuition is a little like a muscle; it needs to be flexed and exercised in order to become stronger. This means you need to practice listening to your inner voice and trusting it blindly, seeing where it takes you. It will get easier over time.

Be Confident in Your Voice

Owning your voice means that you are surer of what you believe. That also means that you're more confident and you're less likely to be taken advantage of by a manipulator. This means being more positive but also examining the things which are important to you, your opinions, your views, and how you see the world. Identify these things and solidify them in your mind. You could also try positive affirmations on a daily basis too, repeating them several times to help give yourself a dose of positive NLP.

Be Open to The Views of Others

Nobody wants to hear that someone in their life is deceiving them, but if a friend or family member sits you down and tells you that they've noticed something a little 'off' about a person in your life and that they're worried they're manipulating you, consider it. Of course, don't blindly believe them, because they could have got it wrong, but be open to it and really examine what you feel and what you believe, beyond the techniques you might have been submitted to.

Nobody you trust and care about is going to tell you this without having real cause to do so.

Always Place Importance on Yourself
Finally, look after number one! Do the things you love, don't stop going out with friends, don't stop exercising, don't stop placing your health as a priority. The moment you do this, the moment you're being sucked into a manipulator's grasp.

Cutting Manipulation Out of Your Life

So, how can you get away from a manipulator? We've talked at length about the whole subject, and if you really do feel that you're in the middle of a negative situation such as this, how can you cut ties and get away?

Walking away from a mental manipulator is very hard and it's likely that you're going to need support from a friend or family member to actually go through with it. Also, remember that you're probably going to question your actions and thoughts several times before and afterward and wonder whether you did the right thing. Always believe that you did the right thing. Walking away from a manipulator is always a positive step, no matter whether it feels that way at the time or not.

A few pieces of advice:

- Leave the situation when they are not around

- Stay with a friend or family member during the aftermath, to give you extra support

- Seek out professional support if you feel you need it

- Block their telephone number and their social media accounts

- Do not talk to them if they find out where you are staying

- Regardless of how many times you wonder if you did the right thing, do not contact them and do not go back to the situation

- Look after yourself and nurture yourself in this time - always know that it will get better and you did a very brave thing by noticing the manipulation and walking away.

The strongest thing you can do in this situation is to walk away with your head held high, no matter what has come before.

Conclusion

And there we have it! We're now at the end of our journey into the rather murky world of mental manipulation. Hopefully, by this point, you will be feeling empowered to either leave a situation that you have identified as manipulative, or you're feeling strong and positive enough to be able to do your best to avoid being a victim in the future.

Manipulation of some kind is everywhere you look, but when it is done with intent it is something which is damaging and needs to be avoided at all costs.

Never be afraid to leave a manipulative situation. You will not change that person, they will never feel bad about it, and none of it is your fault.

All that is left to say is "good luck". Remember, you are stronger than you think, and you can overcome any situation that stands in your way.